Flying Can Be Fun

A GUIDE FOR THE WHITE-KNUCKLED FLYER

Edie Grande

Dyenamiks, Inc.
Middleton, MA

Acknowledgments

I'd like to say thank you to the following people:

Dr. Albert Forgione from the Institute for Psychology of Air Travel in Boston for his support and knowledge.

Nick Wantiez for his technical expertise.

Dad for the paper airplane lessons. Mom, Stephen, Lorna, Nana, Aunty Adele, Julie, Lisa, and Elaine Shaer for their support and encouragement.

Diane Anderson, Deborah Battista, and Kibby Squires for their technical help in preparing the manuscript.

Rex Trailer, Captain Cummings, Joe Veno, Hank Jonas, Eva Lesko, Roberta Rosen, and Kathleen V. Rosenauer for their contributions.

From The Book Department in Brookline: Jim Rigney, my designer; Margaret Kearney and Barbara Ames, my editors; and Mary Day Fewlass, my production and manufacturing coordinator.

And to all my friends for their tips, tricks, and hints to help make flying fun! Martin Duncan Barlow; Bill Lambert, my cartoonist and friend; David Robichaud, my TV news consultant; Jack and Annie Lambert; Debbie and Jack Russo; Keith Jacobson; Robin and Mitchell Dong; Stephen J.; Paula and Steve Copperman; Cheryl Merrill; Jan, Marla, and Erica Pitzi; Larry Lonergan; Phyllis Gutterman; Alison Levins; Valerie Jacoby; Karen Lane; Steve Mayo; and a very special thank you to Mr. Cosmo Nardella.

Credits

Producer: The Book Department, Inc.
Cover Illustration: Joe Veno
Cartoons: William Sterrett Lambert

Library of Congress Catalog Card Number: 90-82697
ISBN: 0-9626980-0-8

Copyright © 1990 by Edytheann Grande

All rights reserved. No part of the material protected by this copyright notice may be reproduced or utilized in any form or by any means, electronic or mechanical, including photocopying, recording, or by any information storage and retrieval system, without the written permission of the copyright owner.

Printed in the United States of America   5 4 3 2 1   95 94 93 92 91 90

Contents

Foreword   1

Chapter One
The Safety of Flying   5
AIR SAFETY — FACT OR FICTION?

Chapter Two
The Aerodynamics of Flying   13
WHAT THE HECK WAS THAT NOISE?

Chapter Three
The Physical Discomforts of Flying   21
OH, MY ACHIN' BACK!

Chapter Four
The Anxiety of Flying   31
PSYCH YOUR PSYCHE!

Chapter Five
Tips for Hassle-Free Flying   43
WORRY NO MORE — LET'S SOAR!

Chapter Six
Flying with Others   59
TAKE MY WIFE, PLEASE!

Chapter Seven
Flying Phobias   67
GOOD NEWS — HELP IS AVAILABLE!

To my love — Peter David Shaer

You are my wings!

Foreword

> "As I entered the concourse, there before me stood the largest plane I had ever seen."

I remember these words well; they were the opening lines of a summer book report I had written when I was ten years old. I got an A on the book report, but I flunked flying for the next twenty-eight years of my life.

You may be saying to yourself, What do I have in common with this person who is an ex-phobic? Just because I have a few drinks on the plane to calm me down or get a little white-knuckled when we hit some turbulence,

> *that does not make me a phobic* — **NO WAY!**

True, but we do have something in common — fear of the unknown. Ignorance is not bliss when you are even the least bit uncomfortable on a plane.

But I didn't write this book for phobics. I wrote it for the 25 million people in the United States who are uncomfortable about flying.

What kind of uncomfortable flyer are you?

1

For example, do you:

- find yourself glued to the television when the news reports a plane crash?
- stay awake all night prior to a flight thinking about what might happen?
- spend the whole flight wondering why take-off was so bumpy?
- worry that those noises mean there is something wrong with the plane?
- feel nauseous and sweaty from beginning to end?

In this book I want to give all of you uncomfortable flyers the information you need to understand what flying is all about. Once you know the mechanics of how the plane stays up there, what all the noises and bumps are, and how to make the experience of flying more comfortable, I think you will find that it is definitely possible to enjoy a flight.

So relax, fasten your seat belt, observe the

NO SMOKING

sign, and get ready to learn.

Chapter One

The Safety of Flying

(AIR SAFETY – FACT OR FICTION?)

We all know that airplanes are here to stay. Those big birds in the sky are the fastest, easiest, and most efficient way to get anywhere in the world. But just how safe is flying? According to the Air Transport Association, it is very safe indeed.

In 1988, the U.S. scheduled airlines had one of their best safety years. Out of nearly 7 million flights of commercial airplanes, with 30 or more seats and carrying over 450 million passengers, there were 3 fatal accidents. Worldwide, the total number of fatalities was 285, of which 270 resulted from the bomb explosion aboard the jet over Lockerbie, Scotland, in December 1988.

Imagine, out of 450 million people only 285 were killed. I know someone who repeats this statistic to herself every time her husband has to fly to a trade show; while it is unfortunate that there are any fatalities, you must admit that these aren't bad odds. In fact, they are quite reassuring when you consider that more than 45,000 people were killed in highway accidents, and another 20,000 died from falls off ladders, down stairs, and even in bathtubs. This information is displayed graphically in the chart on the next page.

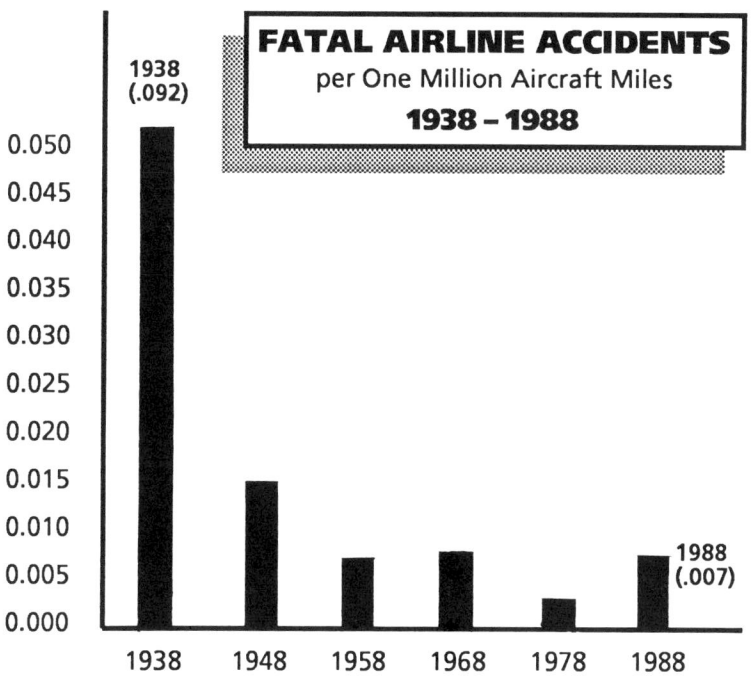

I FEEL A LOT CALMER NOW.

Don't You?

One of my greatest fears about flying used to concern the maintenance of the plane itself. Anyone who's even the least little bit uncomfortable about flying has had misgivings about the professionalism of the ground crew — maybe they had a couple of beers or smoked a joint before

they worked on the plane. The truth is that this just doesn't happen. The Federal Aviation Administration (FAA) sets very strict standards for maintenance crew training, aircraft safety design, and all other matters related to safety.

Thanks to computers, maintenance procedures are very sophisticated these days. Because computers now check all aspects of the aircraft performance during flights, the maintenance crew can identify potential mechanical problems before they become serious. All the operating parameters of an aircraft — things like fuel consumption, engine temperatures, and cabin pressure — are monitored constantly by the flight crew. Again, this is so the maintenance crew can spot potential problems before they become real problems. Furthermore, airlines are spending increasing amounts of money to maintain the aircraft. From 1981 to 1988, industry maintenance expenditures rose 55 percent for a total of $55 billion.

The different components of an airplane are becoming more reliable all the time. For example, Rolls Royce recently reported that one of its jet engines completed 20,000 flight hours of uninterrupted flying, which is the equivalent of 10 million air miles. The engine was monitored constantly and showed no signs of deteriorating performance. Can any U. S. car manufacturer make the same claim?

In the early days of aviation, after a certain number of hours, engines were taken apart and checked for problems. Today, such nondestructive techniques as x-ray, ultrasound, fluorescent penetrant eddy current, and magnetic particle methods are used to find defects. Think of it as Superman looking into an airplane engine with his x-ray vision and telling the maintenance crew when he sees something that needs to be repaired.

The FAA allows airlines to fly if certain items on a plane are inoperative, as long as there is a backup, the item is optional, or the item is there solely for passenger comfort. So, if your chair doesn't go all the way back or your reading light doesn't work, there's no reason to worry about what else isn't working. The airlines will not postpone maintenance on items related to the safe operation of the airplane — such items have to be fixed before the next flight.

There is no question...

SAFETY IS #1

Forget about safety for a minute and think about the cost of a new airplane — *tens of millions of dollars*! If you were an airline executive, you'd make sure these expensive babies were kept in tip-top shape. From a dollars-and-cents point of view, running a safe airline is simply good business.

All the effort that goes into keeping those big birds in the sky isn't the only reassuring news. You will also be happy to hear that getting to be a pilot and staying a pilot are extremely difficult. The airlines hire only the most qualified pilots, and once hired, pilots become part of the most strictly controlled profession in the United States.

Consider for a moment these facts:

The average flight time of a newly hired pilot in 1988 was over 3,000 hours, and the majority of these pilots gained their flight experience in the military or as commuter or corporate pilots.

The airlines require prospective pilots to take psychological aptitude tests in addition to a stringent medical exam. These tests, along with several flight simulation evaluations, are used to screen out the top 10 to 15 percent of applicants.

Even after a pilot has been selected (from among approximately 12,000 applicants), the FAA requires that additional, intensive training be completed. It doesn't stop there.

All pilots are required to have complete medical exams twice yearly.

All pilots and flight engineers must complete specified recurrent training every year, and captains must complete some elements of this training every six months.

You're in good hands with these guys!

Chapter Two

The Aerodynamics of Flying

(WHAT THE HECK WAS THAT NOISE?)

Large and small planes alike use the same principles to get off the ground: power, lift, and direction. All of these together enable the plane to become airborne.

Power (the engines)

When the pilot flips the ignition switch, here's what happens:

- Air gets sucked into the front of the plane and is compressed by several spinning blades (like a fan). This makes the air hot.
- The air mixes with fuel, which causes the mixture (at this point it's not air anymore but more like some sort of gas) to burn and expand.
- Gas gets pushed into a turbine wheel.
- Finally, the gas is pushed out of the plane.

The important thing to remember is that during the entire process, the air/gas is moving faster and faster, with more and more power, so that by the time the airplane is moving down the runway and is just about to lift off the ground, it's moving at a speed of about 180 miles per hour.

Lift (the wings)

Once the plane has the power to fly, this is how it gets off the ground:

- The pilot eases the control column back, which causes the nose of the plane to lift upward.
- As the plane points up, air gets under the wings and the plane moves upward even faster and easier.
- The air under the wings gives it the push to keep moving upward.

(Remember when you were little and you stuck your hand out of the window as you were riding in a car? If you tilted your palm upward, the air pushed your whole hand up — just like a plane.)

Direction (the rudder)

Now that the plane is flying, how does it get you from Cincinnati to St. Moritz? An airplane has a rudder for control. The rudder is located on the tail and moves back and forth. Ailerons are movable surfaces located on the wings. They turn the plane smoothly. Climbing and descending are done by horizontal tail surfaces called elevators. The pilot has control over all these movements from the cockpit.

BEFORE TAKEOFF

The flight crew begins checking out the plane an hour before takeoff. First, the pilot does a visual inspection of the outside of the plane, checking all systems. Inside the cockpit, the pilot uses a printed checklist to check instruments, systems, and computers. After receiving a weather briefing and filing a flight plan, the pilot calls for IFR clearance. The IFR clearance is read back for the pilot to double-check for any errors. The air traffic control tower instructs the plane to go to the end of the runway to a designated area. (Commercial planes are cleared to a certain point.) When the plane is next in line, the tower clears it for takeoff. All communication between the pilot and tower is repeated and acknowledged — there are no misunderstandings.

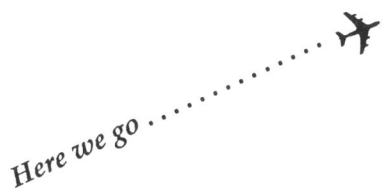

TAKEOFF

Now we are ready for the takeoff. And yes, the plane does make odd noises.

The engine revs up, and the airplane starts taxiing down the runway.

- **Squeak-squeak-squeak, groan-groan-groan:** The structural body of the plane is bending and twisting — perfectly normal.
- *HMMMMMMMMMM, HMMMMMMMM:* The flaps are going down for takeoff.
- **ROOOOOOOO, ROOOOOOO:** The plane rolls and bumps on the runway as it revs up.

15

The airplane's wings bend and sway as the plane shakes and rolls down the runway— perfectly normal. When the airplane reaches rotation speed, the tail goes down and the wings go up. Once there is a sufficient angle between the wind and the plane, the plane leaves the ground.

- **ROAAAAAAAR, ROAAAAAAAR:** The landing gear is coming up and the landing gear door closes.
- **WHINE-WHINE-WHINE:** The flaps are being adjusted as the plane climbs. Once the plane climbs to cruise altitude, the flaps are all the way up. The plane is in cruise configuration.

Now that you understand what happens during takeoff, let's recap all those noises. As the airplane taxies down the runway, the **ROOOOOOOO** noise is the engine getting warmed up. All the little squeaks and groans are normal too — something called structural deflection causes them. While you are taxiing, you'll also hear a loud **HMMMMM**, which is the wing flaps going up. Just as you're leaving the ground, you'll hear a **ROAAAAAAAR** noise. This is all the air whooshing underneath the wings, and as we now know, this is how the plane gets off the ground.

LANDING

It's time to land and more noises again.

- Engine revs down twice — **WHRRRRRR, WHRRRRRR.**
- Engine revs up — **ROAAAAAAR, ROAAAAAAR, ROAAAAAAR.**
- At destination engine revs down.
- Flaps **WHRRRRRR** — landing gear is down.

- **THUMP** — landing gear is locked into place and there may be a feeling of movement.
- Heading into approach — landing strip looks like gum wrapper at this height.
- Plane is fully controlled by radar.
- Pilot may rev at this point — plane may bounce around.
- **THUMP** — we've landed.
- ROAAAAAAR of thrust reversers — squeak of brakes — spoilers stand up on wings to stop lift.

When the plane gets ready to land, some of the same noises as in takeoff occur but in a different order. The first sound you hear that tells you the pilot is getting ready to land the plane aside from the flight attendant telling you to fasten your safety belts is the *WHRRRRRR* of the wing flaps coming down. Once you've landed, you'll hear the ROAAAAAAR noise, but this time it is caused by the thrust reversers, which are used to slow the plane down. You will hear some squeaking noises, but they only mean that the pilot is using the brakes to slow the plane down even more.

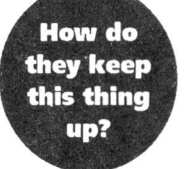

MYTHS: THE TRUTH WILL SET YOU FREE

Let's review several myths that most uncomfortable flyers believe can happen once you're in the air.

1. The chances of a mid-air collision are pretty good.

Actually, the chances of a mid-air collision are very, very slim because all pilots file flight plans before they take off. They file these plans with air traffic controllers, who can then see if any other planes might be flying in the same airspace at the same time. Also, planes flying east to west travel at an altitude designated in even increments, and planes flying west to east travel in altitudes of odd increments.

2. *Turbulence will cause a plane to crash.*

Planes are designed to withstand enormous amounts of turbulence. Structural tests create conditions so extreme that even Mother Nature couldn't duplicate them. The tests simulate air pockets, which are really gusts or puffs of air that move a plane, and windshears, uneven gusty winds that change direction and force. Incidentally, any air that is not perfectly smooth is called turbulence. Choppiness occurs in unstable air. So, remember, when it's gusty on the way to the airport, expect some choppiness for a few minutes after takeoff. Clear air turbulence can also occur. This is when two air streams traveling at different speeds converge. The air becomes choppy and disturbed where they blend — sort of like two streams coming together into a river. So, don't worry — a bump is a bump is a bump!

3. *If a plane flies through a thunderstorm, lightning can hit the plane and everyone will be electrocuted.*

Not true for two reasons: First, air traffic control uses radar to pick up thunderstorms, and pilots are then instructed to fly under or around them. Second, an airplane is a completely bonded metallic conductor, which means that it's impossible for lightning to penetrate or disable a plane. The fact is, you are much, much safer in an airplane than anywhere else during a thunderstorm! Storms are uncomfortable but not unsafe, and pilots usually avoid them.

4. *If anything goes wrong with any part of the engine, the risk of the plane crashing increases tenfold.*

Wrong! Planes are designed to simulate the worst possible conditions, including engine failure. If they lose

an engine, they can still fly on the remaining engines. If they have three engines, they can fly on two. If only one engine is working, a plane still has directional control. Even if all the engines are out, a commercial airliner can coast up to 250 miles. A plane just doesn't drop out of the sky.

5. *Delayed takeoff is not a good sign — there's probably something wrong with the plane.*

Ninety-nine percent of the time, nothing is wrong. There can be several reasons for a delay, including that the pilot is waiting for clearance from the air traffic control tower because other planes have been scheduled to land first.

Don't Listen To RUMORS

Chapter Three

The Physical Discomforts of Flying

(OH, MY ACHIN' BACK!)

TO SLEEP, PER CHANCE TO DREAM

If you're like most people, sometimes you are able to fall asleep during a flight and sometimes you are not. The following tips will help ensure that you are always able to sleep when you want to:

- **Cut out coffee and tea.** Instead, drink whole milk. The sedative-like effect of tryptophane, an essential amino acid found in milk, seems to have a calming effect on most people.
- **You might try a glass of brandy, wine, or other liquor, but be careful to limit yourself.** (The effects of alcohol will be described later in this chapter.)
- **Make yourself as comfortable as possible in your seat.** Don't be shy about asking for more pillows, and if the seat next to you is empty, pull up the arm rest and stretch out.
- **Bring eyeshades and earplugs and use them.**

> *You got your earplugs in?*............
> # Whadayasay?

- **Try to relax — don't worry if you don't fall into a deep sleep.** Relaxing your body and taking naps are very beneficial.
- **Listen to a relaxation tape or some mellow music.**
- **Halcion (triazolam) is a new prescription sleeping aid in the bensodiazepine family.** Unlike other prescription sleeping drugs, Halcion washes out of your system quickly so you won't be left with a hung-over feeling. Talk to your doctor about this drug. Preliminary tests seem to indicate it's good for treating sleep problems for travelers and perhaps even the effects of jet lag.

SWEET DREAMS

DEALING WITH PHYSICAL DISCOMFORTS

Dry Skin

Increased pressure and low humidity combine to provide a very dry environment in the airplane cabin. Cabin humidity can range from 0 to 25 percent. While there's nothing we can do to change the dry atmosphere in flight, we can prepare for it ahead of time by limiting our intake of coffee and alcohol.

Once on the plane, walk to the galley every hour for a glass of water. Carry moisturizer with you for your hands, mineral water to spritz on your face, and lip balm to prevent chapping. If the lining of your nose becomes chapped, irritated, or cracked, put a dab of Vaseline in your nose and pinch your nostrils together to lubricate them. If you wear contact lenses, take them out during the flight and use eye drops to soothe your eyes if they become irritated.

After you land and are settled in somewhere, try to allow yourself time to take a shower. Moisturize your face and body completely again. If your eyes are puffy, lie down with a cool compress or place eye gel on your eyes. Drink six to eight glasses of water for a few days after the flight to replace the fluid you lost.

> **KEEP YOURSELF WELL LUBRICATED**

Foot Problems

Swollen feet are sometimes a problem. Take an extra pair of shoes one size larger than your normal shoe size. That way if your feet begin to get puffy, you will have a comfortable pair of shoes to wear. Fortunately, many shoe manufacturers are now offering shoes with soles that are soft, comfortable, and easy on the feet.

Some people complain of foot cramps. Help manipulate the joints and loosen tight foot muscles by making a fist with your foot; then slowly curl the toes inward. Repeat this action several times with each foot.

Now, place your feet on the floor slightly apart. Lift your heels off the floor and hold this position for 5 seconds. Then, place your heels back on the floor and lift your toes up. Hold this position for 5 seconds. Repeat five times.

You will find that these two exercises will increase the circulation in your feet and legs and reduce muscle stiffness. Try to do the routine every half hour or so.

Muscle Stiffness and Fatigue

Fatigue and muscle soreness can be uncomfortable and annoying. The best remedy is exercise, and lots of exercises can be done right in your seat. Do also make sure you get up and stretch your entire body by walking around the plane at least once an hour. You can be doing that at the same time you are heading to the galley for your hourly glass of water.

The following exercise will relieve cramped muscles and allow you to stretch your whole body. Sit up straight in your seat. Clasp your hands and hold your arms over your head with the palms facing upward. Stretch your clasped arms to the left and hold for 3 seconds. Then, stretch to the right and hold for another 3 seconds. Lower your arms.

STRETCH THOSE AIR-BORNE MUSCLES

Next, raise a knee to your chest and hold your hands around it, pointing your foot at the same time. Hold this position for 4 seconds. Repeat with your other knee.

For the last exercise, hold on to the arms of your seat, press against the back of the seat, stiffen your arms, and tense your legs. Hold for 4 seconds. Now let your legs, arms, shoulders, and neck relax. Take a few deep breaths, inhaling and exhaling slowly.

Repeat these three exercises once every half hour.

EXERCISING CAN BE FUN

Especially on a plane.

Back Pain

If you are prone to back problems, traveling on planes can really aggravate them. During the flight, try to avoid sitting for longer than a half hour, and make sure you stretch, stretch, stretch! Try putting a pillow in the hollow of your lower back — this will give your back some extra support. Whatever you do, don't slouch in your seat! Ask for an aisle seat so you will have more room to stretch out.

At the airport, use a cart to carry your luggage or have a porter do it. Buy suitcases with wheels or invest in a folding luggage trolley. If you absolutely have to deal with your own luggage, slide it or push it across the floor — don't carry it. Imagine lying in bed in a hotel room for two days just because you lifted your suitcase the wrong way!

If you do suffer from back trouble, ask your doctor about taking analgesics or anti–inflammatory drugs. You might also use a counter-irritant, such as Ben-Gay.

Krick in your back?

ALL GONE

Air Circulation (Too Hot or Too Cold)

If you fall asleep in your seat, you might wake up feeling like you're in Siberia. The best way to feel comfortable is to wear layers of clothing that you can add or remove. If the air vent is blowing arctic air on you and the plane isn't full, ask the flight attendant if you can move to a more comfortable spot. Or, if you're too warm, ask the flight attendant to turn up the air circulation system — it's not usually turned up full blast. The air won't get colder, but more air will blow on you.

If heat tends to bother you, ask to sit away from the galley.

JET LAG

Jet lag is not just simple fatigue; it is a disturbance of our internal clocks. Flying across time zones disturbs our natural body rhythm. Flying west tends to be harder on air travelers than flying east, and crossing more than five time zones on a flight is hard on almost all travelers.

Researchers now know that sunlight shifts the body clock by suppression of the hormone Melantonin. People who cross up to six time zones and are traveling east should spend time outside in the morning. If you are traveling west and cross five or six time zones, spend time outside in the evening light before dusk.

If you just came in on the Red-Eye overnight flight from California to Boston, arriving early in the morning, try to stay up and go to bed around 8 or 9 p.m. local time. Or, if you hit the West Coast at 6 p.m., stay up until 11 p.m., and the next day you'll be on new time. If your trip is longer than 24 hours, before you leave adjust your watch and your schedule to the destination time.

MOTION SICKNESS

Nobody is quite sure what causes motion sickness, but some air travelers definitely suffer from it. For the smoothest possible ride, choose a seat over the wings where there is less vibration and avoid the tail section where you get the bumpiest ride. Turn the overhead vent toward you and do not sit in the smoking section.

Some physicians will prescribe a dime-sized patch that is applied to the skin behind the ears and releases measured doses of Scopolamine over 72 hours. Consult your doctor about using the patch and about any possible side effects.

Dramamine, an over-the-counter motion sickness drug, can be bought at a drug store and usually in the airport terminal. Check with your doctor for any possible side effects.

Interestingly, powdered ginger root has been tested and found to be very effective in reducing motion sickness. Ginger root is taken in capsule form and can be purchased at health food stores. Check with the health food store for the correct dosage.

A do-it-yourself remedy is to lay your arm flat and then press the Nei-Kuan acupressure point, which is located three finger breadths above the major crease of the wrist. Within a minute or so the nausea should pass. Since this remedy isn't permanent, you might try an acupressure motion sickness band, which also applies pressure to the Nei-Kuan acupressure point. Originally developed for sea sickness, it has been found to be effective for air sickness as well. You can order this wristband, called Travelgarde, from:

>   Marine Logic
>   400 Australian Avenue
>   West Palm Beach, FL 33401
>   (407) 832-5112

A friend recently told me that when she got very nauseous on a flight, the flight attendant suggested she sit up straight and push her head back into the seat and chew on a piece of ice.
.........IT WORKED!

Ear-Popping Pain

A plane's air supply is condensed or pressurized, and one of the common side effects of this is popping ears or ear pain. To prevent your ears from popping when the plane ascends or descends, chew gum, swallow hard, or suck on hard candy. If this doesn't work, pinch your nostrils, close your mouth, and gently blow, puffing out your cheeks. Some people suggest using an over-the-counter drug like Neo–Synephrine or Afrin. Use the spray before getting on the plane and, if the flight is longer than four hours, spray again before starting the descent. Remember, on long flights the descent can begin an hour before scheduled landing time, so ask the flight attendant for landing information.

If you have a cold or ear trouble, most doctors would advise you to postpone the flight. Infection causes swelling around the flutter valve of the Eustacian tube in the ear, making it difficult for the valve to relieve the air-pressure changes that accompany descent, so you may be unusually uncomfortable.

An aerodynamics engineer I know has a good suggestion if you have to travel with a cold or if your ears are sensitive. Just before descent begins, go to the bathroom, take two styrofoam cups and put steaming hot paper towels in them, return to your seat, and cover both ears with the cups. You may look silly, but this routine works.

PLAN AHEAD

Most of us don't think about our aches and pains until we have been sitting in our seat for a while. Take the time when you plan your trip to think about what is going to bother you — your back, your feet, your ears, your stomach, your skin?

Consult your doctor about serious problems that might require prescription medicine. You might also check your local drugstore and some of the popular mail order catalogues for other items that will help you deal with those aches and pains. *Herrington Catalogue* is one excellent mail order source of exciting travel gadgets designed to make flying more comfy. To receive the catalogue, call (603) 437-4939.

Chapter Four

The Anxiety of Flying

PSYCH YOUR PSYCHE!

DEALING WITH ANXIETY

Anxiety about flying can attack anyone at any time. Even after flying comfortably for years, you can suddenly become nervous. This anxiety is normal, so relax and don't let the irrational thoughts overwhelm you. Stop and think for a minute — did something major happen in your life recently? Divorce, separation, marriage, birth, change of residence, illness, or death of a loved one? All of these things, believe it or not, can trigger white-knuckled flying. If you find yourself suddenly anxious on a plane, review the last year of your life and calm down — all major changes, good or bad, can bring on some anxiety.

Anticipation is usually the worst part of anxiety. Depending on how active your imagination is, getting ready for a flight can work you into a frenzy and you start torturing yourself from the moment you know you're going to be flying somewhere. You are not alone in these feelings.

Dr. Albert Forgione, the doctor who teaches the Fear of Flying course at Logan International Airport in Boston, believes that nutrition plays a major role in how we handle stress. Dr. Forgione suggests you rid your body of all sugar and caffeine a week before the flight. Cutting down on caffeine will decrease muscle tension and slow down your heart rate. Vitamin C also reduces stress, and Dr. Forgione suggests that you consult your doctor about using vitamins to combat pre-flight stress.

Dr. Forgione recommends the following diet to help relax your body before flying:

- **Breakfast** — Have a good breakfast — some meat or eggs to give you protein, toast with margarine or butter, and orange juice.
- **Mid-morning** — Instead of a sweet roll and coffee (refined sugar jolts your system), munch on some nuts, raisins, cheese and crackers, or grapes (the natural sugar in fruit helps your body relax). If you can't cut out coffee altogether, try to make every other cup decaf.
- **Lunch** — More protein (a tuna fish sandwich, for example).
- **Mid-afternoon** — A piece of fruit (remember to have natural sugar instead of refined sugar) and some protein.
- **Dinner** — Another source of protein (meat, fish, etc.). Take it easy on the carbohydrates like noodles, potatoes, and bread.
- **Before bed** — More protein.

NERVOUS?

WHO? ...ME? WHO? ...ME?
WHO? .....ME? WHO? .....ME?
WHO? .....ME?
WHO? .....ME?

RELAXATION EXERCISES

Anticipating an event we find unpleasant causes more stress in our bodies than almost anything else. Being scared makes the muscles tighten up. Once your body is tensed like this, you tend to overact to noise and other external stimulation. This is something all white-knuckled flyers need to be aware of. However, there are several relaxation techniques that can relieve this kind of stress. Practice them all to see what works best for you.

Breathing Correctly

Correct breathing can do a lot to settle those butterflies in your stomach. As we get older, it seems that we learn some bad habits in terms of our breathing techniques. For one thing, we become shallow breathers. Think about it — breathe normally for a minute. Does your chest move up and down? Probably not. Now try this: Lean back in your chair at a 45-degree angle. Put one hand on your chest and one on your stomach. Breathe in slowly and let your belly fill up with air. As this happens, the hand on your stomach will be pushed out. The hand on your chest should also move. You should feel the muscles in your stomach moving as you inhale. Now, gently exhale. This is diaphragmatic, or belly, breathing. Students of Yoga and Zen are taught to breathe this way. Diaphragmatic breathing slows the heartbeat, lowers blood pressure, and relaxes the body.

TAKE A DEEP BREATH
(sssssssuuuuuuuuupp)
FILL THOSE LUNGS UP

It's hard to feel nervous on a plane when your body is relaxed by diaphragmatic breathing. Take about 10 deep, slow breaths and you will feel the tension in your body fade away.

Progressive Muscle Relaxation

In this exercise, you will tighten and then relax every major muscle group in your body. Start at the bottom and work your way up: tighten all the muscles in your feet and count to five as you keep them tensed. Then, as you count to five again, relax all the muscles in your feet and count to five as you keep them relaxed. Make sure you feel them becoming looser and looser, just as you concentrated on feeling them tighten up. Next, tighten and relax the muscles in your thighs, your buttocks, your arms, your shoulders, your neck, and finally your face.

Jamming Exercise

Breathe deeply as the plane is readying for takeoff. As the plane starts taxiing down the runway, sit compactly in your seat, without touching the sides of the seat. Dig your heels into the floor and lean way back into the seat. Keep breathing diaphragmatically. Actual takeoff will last from 35 to 45 seconds — you should be digging your heels in, leaning back, and breathing deeply for the whole takeoff.

This was one of the most valuable bits of advice I learned from Dr. Forgione's Fear of Flying class. It really helps to relieve the anxiety of takeoff. By the time you've finished the exercise, you are in the air.

THOUGHT-STOPPING

Another technique to help manage the frightening and seemingly uncontrollable thoughts that race through your head is called "thought-stopping." When you start to feel the "bad" thoughts, imagine a big stop sign looming up in front of your face. Silently scream "STOP!" This sounds weird, but it works. It will take your mind off the negative thoughts.

IMAGERY

My brother Stephen once told me that when he gets on a plane, he puts on the headphones, closes his eyes, relaxes, and makes believe he's on a bus. That's not as funny as it sounds — using imagery to fool yourself into forgetting your frightening, negative thoughts really works.

✌ **LEAVE THE DRIVING TO US**

Reading, listening to tapes, watching the movie, talking to others around you are all things that will help pass the time. They will also distract you from the fact that you are in an airplane. Buy a magazine you might not usually read at home — something that will really hold your attention — *Playgirl*, *Playboy*, the *National Enquirer*!

ANTI-ANXIETY DRUGS

Some excellent anti-anxiety drugs are available on the market today. They are not to be confused with tranquilizers; rather, these anti-anxiety drugs deal specifically with reducing anxiety. Two of the most widely used anti-anxiety drugs are Ativan and Xanax. Talk to your doctor about possibly using these. I've used Xanax and found it has helped me enormously.

JUST A WORD ABOUT ALCOHOL

Most white-knuckled flyers have a drink during the flight to calm themselves. Alcohol, in moderation, can mellow you out, but if you are very nervous, too much alcohol can turn the flight into a disaster. The Committee on Alcoholism and Drug Dependence of the American Medical Association describes the psychological effects of alcohol this way:

> **Ingestion** of small quantities of alcohol usually reduces the feelings of anxiety and worry and causes a mild but general reduction of inhibition. If drinking is continued beyond euphoria and exhilaration, dysfunctional reactions such as aggression, antagonism, depression and psychosis may appear, as well as disruption of speech and memory.

Remember, two drinks in a plane are equivalent to three on the ground. Feeling anxious and nervous on the plane will mask how intoxicated you may be getting. Once you hit the ground, the effects of the alcohol will become apparent. There is nothing more embarrassing than having to be helped from the plane because you are too drunk to walk. And then don't forget about the hangover which will follow.

ONE OR TWO WILL DO
That's All
If not at all.

SOMETIMES THERE ARE OTHER FEARS.......

By the way, some people aren't actually uncomfortable about being in a plane, or flying; they're uncomfortable about being confined in a small place, or are afraid of heights (or elevators). A Fear of Flying course can help you deal with these types of fears, as well as the fear of flying. Please see Chapter 7 for specific information on courses given in the United States.

Chapter Five
Tips for Hassle-Free Flying

WORRY NO MORE — LET'S SOAR!

TRAVEL TIPS

Special Meals

Did you know that special meals are available on flights for people who have dietary, health, or religious concerns? Whatever your preference, the following categories of meals can be ordered at the time you make your flight reservation:

- low-calorie
- low-cholesterol
- vegetarian
- bland
- salt-free
- kosher

Promotional Fares

From time to time airlines run money-saving promotions. The two most common are APEX for international flights and SUPERSAVER for domestic flights. Although savings can be substantial, there are certain restrictions, including the following:

- Tickets must be purchased 21 to 30 days before departure.
- The minimum stay is usually 7 days.
- There is a penalty for changes or cancellations.
- For the best savings, plan to depart midweek.

International Travel Packages

Low fares are available if you book air and hotel ahead. International packages are also available at reduced rates. If you travel as part of a group of ten or more, you may also be eligible for special, lower rates. Talk to your travel agent.

Charters

While you can expect savings on nonscheduled flights, be prepared for some hassles. For example, you might have to leave with only two days notice, and there is usually a penalty for cancellation. For protection against cancellation, make your check payable to the tour's escrow account. Put flight details on the front of your check and write "for deposit only" on the back of the check.

Fare Codes

Many different fares are available on every flight depending on when you fly (midweek, weekend, high, low, or shoulder season), where you sit (first class, business class, or coach), and how far ahead you book your flight (Apex or special fares). Excursion rates have certain restrictions attached to your fare; tour-based rates are dependent on your booking an entire package with the airline. The table opposite further defines the air fare codes the airlines use to code your ticket.

FARE CODE CHART

Code **Translation**

X — Midweek travel — flights Monday through Thursday

W or Z — Weekend travel — flights Friday through Sunday

H — High season — the most expensive time to fly — holiday periods are usually blacked out

L — Low season — least expensive fares (dates and destinations determine price)

F — First class — most expensive seating, but also most comfortable, offering some amenities (often "better meals" or free headsets)

Y — Coach — less comfortable seating but you arrive at your destination the same time first-class travelers do

J or C — Business class — amenities and fare price usually between first class and coach

YN — Night coach — coach fare, but flying at night is less expensive

FN — Night first class — same as first class, but a night flight

B or BE — Excursion — some restrictions on dates and destinations may apply

AP or AB — Apex — usually involves advance ticket purchase — this code is used primarily for international flights

IT — Tour-based fare — refers to a special fare offered by an airline only if a tour package (air and land transportation) is booked

NR — Nonrefundable — many low-cost fares are available because the tickets are nonrefundable

Fare Protection Insurance

With fare protection insurance, you can travel at a lower price on tickets purchased in advance, even if the fare goes up. If the fare goes down, you can obtain a refund and repurchase the ticket.

Trip Cancellation Insurance

You can buy trip cancellation insurance from your travel agent or Access America (800-851-2800). This is good in case of illness, but find out from your travel agent the exact limitations on the coverage.

Getting Bumped

Getting bumped because of overbooking is aggravating for some air travelers and a bonus for others. If you get bumped, the airline will fly you on the next available flight. In addition, some airlines will give you a free round-trip ticket to anywhere in their domestic system. For those who do not have to adhere to a prearranged schedule, the free ticket is a nice incentive to give up a seat. But if you are unhappy about getting bumped, at the very least demand boarding compensation dollars and ask for a meal chit if the delay means missing a meal. If bumping causes an overnight delay, the airline may put you up in a hotel or motel free.

Connecting for an International Flight

When traveling from one U.S. city to another to catch an overseas flight, show your foreign ticket to a ticket agent and save the 8 percent federal tax on the airline. Ask your travel agent for details when booking your flight.

Car Rentals and Courtesy Buses

If you are going to need a car rental, ask the airline reservationist about special car rental rates that might be available to airline passengers. Also inquire about the availability of a courtesy bus to the hotel where you are staying. Before making reservations for a trip, call the 800 free directory assistance number (800-555-1212) to find out if your airline hotel or rent-a-car company has a toll-free number. Most do.

HEALTH HOT LINES

Before you take off on a business trip or vacation, make sure you have these important phone numbers with you:

- **The State Department Overseas Citizens Emergency Center**

  Mon. to Fri., 8:15 a.m. to 10 p.m. (EST)

  (202) 647-5225

  The State Department's main concern is the health and political safety of American citizens. The department keeps up-to-date information on epidemics and unstable political situations. The State Department can also help U.S. citizens return in emergency situations. Carry this number when you travel.

- **American Express Global Assist**

  24 hours a day

  (800) 554-2639

  If you are an American Express cardholder, use this number for questions on visa requirements and weather conditions. You can also use this number for obtaining emergency prescriptions that have to be shipped from the United States, or if you need to have an emergency message sent back home.

- **United States Public Health Service**

  Monitored and updated continuously, the U.S. Public Health Service provides information on epidemics and other health risks. Contact any of the following regional offices:

  New York
  (718) 917-1685
  San Francisco
  (415) 876-2872
  Miami
  (305) 526-2910
  Seattle
  (206) 442-4519
  Chicago
  (312) 686-2150
  Honolulu
  (808) 541-2552
  Los Angeles
  (213) 215-2363

- **Compuserve**

  Personal Computer users can obtain travel advisories through Compuserve using the command **GO DOSO**.

MEDICAL TIPS

Refilling Prescriptions

If you are in a foreign country and find yourself in need of a doctor, call the U.S. Embassy and ask for the name of a reputable physician. The concierge at your hotel will be happy to help, but foreign doctors aren't always up to U.S. standards. A lot of prescription drugs are sold over the counter in foreign countries, but the packaging is different and you may unwittingly take the wrong dosage. Know the generic name of your drug and the correct dosage. Before you leave home, ask your doctor to write up a duplicate, legible prescription for you and make sure it contains generic and trade names of the drug and correct dosage. If you are going to be in a country such as Greece or China where the alphabet is different, bring a translation of your prescription from home.

Immunization

Update your immunizations, especially if you are traveling to an exotic destination. Make sure you are protected against the following diseases:

- polio
- measles
- tetanus
- diptheria
- influenza

I read somewhere that of the 8 million people who travel to third-world countries each year, only half seek medical advice. That statistic, coupled with the fact that most people between the ages of 40 and 60 have let their immunizations lapse, can turn a vacation into a disaster. Be sure you get up-to-date immunization information and allow plenty of time to get any necessary immunizations. Some series of shots can take several weeks. Ask your doctor.

Taking a Medical Passport

If you are a person with a chronic disease, carry a medical history, including a list of medications that you take. You can get this information from your doctor before leaving. Heart patients should take a copy of their EKG. If you need a blood transfusion while abroad and are in Africa or a third-world country, try to get airlifted to a western European country. In an emergency, ask for someone you are traveling with and trust to donate blood for your transfusion.

TRAVEL MEDICAL KIT

adhesive dressing for small kids	washcloth
ace bandage for sprains	ice pack
calamine lotion or baking soda	sterile gauze
liquid antiseptic	heating pad
adhesive tape and scissors	aspirin or substitute
antiseptic ointment	tweezer
insect repellant	needle
rubbing alcohol	flashlight

Always Better to Be Prepared

TIPS FOR LOOKING YOUR BEST

The most sensible way to take a long flight if you have an early meeting or are meeting your beau at Heathrow is to board the airplane wearing as little makeup as possible. Prescriptives Cosmetics has an in-flight cream to keep your skin supple and moist. Apply this cream at the beginning of the flight. Then, relax and drink plenty of water. An hour before landing, head for the lavatory.

After 8 hours on a nonstop flight, we could all use a little sprucing up. Here are some tips for the ladies on looking as fresh as possible:

- Wash off the Prescriptives Flight Cream with a steaming hot facecloth (carry it in a plastic self-sealing bag).
- Leave the facecloth on for a few minutes.
- Wash your face with cleanser. Use toner and moisturizer (you will need lots of moisturizer on your face and hands).
- Brush your teeth, use deodorant, and splash on your favorite cologne.
- Do a complete makeup.
- If you wear contacts, put them in (wear glasses on the plane, as they are gentler on the eyes).

And let's not leave out the gents. Here are some tips for them:

- About an hour before landing use the lavatory to freshen up.
- Bring a small travel kit with a toothbrush, disposable razor, shaving cream, after-shave lotion, soap, moisturizer, and deodorant.

TRAVEL DOCUMENTS

Passport

The basic and most important travel document is a passport. It identifies you as an American citizen. Getting a passport is not difficult. Passports are issued by the U.S. Passport Agencies located in large cities, some major post offices, and the clerks of federal and state courts. Bring with you your birth certificate and two small photos (not more than six months old). Adult passports are valid for ten years and the fee is $42. Passports for minors are valid for 5 years and cost $27.

Visa

A visa is a foreign country's permission, stamped in your passport, allowing you to enter that country. Visas can be obtained from the Visa Service or the foreign consulate in the United States (except for Soviet-Bloc countries). Dates of expiration vary from country to country.

Proof of Vaccination

Since we live in the world's healthiest country, most of the foreign countries you visit won't ask for vaccination proof. Make sure you ask your travel agent or airlines for the handful of countries where smallpox, cholera, and yellow fever are a threat. The international yellow fever vaccination certificate form may be obtained from the U.S. Public Health Service and at U.S. passport offices. Yellow fever shots are provided by the U.S. Public Health Service. Your own doctor can give the other shots.

AVOIDING AIRPORT HASSLES

Most major airports are situated in densely populated urban areas. Remember, half the aggravation of flying is getting to the airport, and if you're a white-knuckled flyer, you need to avoid situations that bring about extra stress. With a little thought, you can avoid most hassles by organizing your time.

The busiest times in major airports are from 7:30 a.m. to 9:30 a.m. and from 5:30 p.m. to 7:30 p.m. Those times, of course, are also the peak hours for the commuter work traffic. Never underestimate traffic problems. As Murphy said, "If something can go wrong, it will." Be sure to allow a realistic amount of "extra" time to get through tunnels, over bridges, and through toll booths on your way to the airport.

The whole idea is to stay as calm as possible before your flight. Better you should spend a few minutes at the airport doing diaphragmatic breathing and a few relaxing exercises waiting for your plane to be called than blowing a gasket sitting in traffic thinking you'll miss the plane. Try this. It really works!

Plan on arriving at the airport at least an hour ahead of departure. You should have already bought your ticket and picked it up from a travel agent or had it sent out by the airlines. Checking in will be faster if you have purchased your ticket ahead of time. Give your bags to a sky cap when you arrive at the terminal so your bags can be ticketed before you get in line.

Here's another hassle-free tip: Buy your ticket, rent the car, and book hotels through an agent. It really saves a lot of time and phone calls.

While you are waiting at the airport, buy a little booklet on your destination and pass the time by planning your first day. It will keep your mind off the flight.

TIPS FOR GOING THROUGH AIRPORT SECURITY

- Ask your airline how much extra time to allow for security procedures.
- Be able to vouch for all of your luggage — don't take anyone else's packages.
- Keep your bags with you at all times; unattended luggage or packages could be lost, stolen, or damaged by airport security personnel.
- Loosely pack your carry-ons in case you have to open them.
- Keep your film in a special lead bag in case the inspector puts the bag through the x-ray machine.
- Keep electronic devices and video cameras available for hand inspection.
- Don't wear heavy jewelry or belts or carry a lot of keys when you pass through metal detectors.
- And careful — no jokes about bombs or terrorists. Even pranksters are taken seriously these days. No one — security people or passengers — wants to take the slightest chance when it comes to airport security.

PACKING TIPS

My best tips on packing come from a friend who is a frequent flyer. She says to avoid the hassle of packing:

- Make a list of all the clothes you will need.
- Lay the items out on your bed.
- Put together fast, easy outfits, made of fabrics that pack well and don't need to be ironed.
- Limit shoes and bags by interchanging them.
- Choose jewelry that you can interchange with lots of outfits.

Remember, unless you're heading for Pago Pago (where one bikini is all you need), there are stores should you forget anything

If it's cold, take a raincoat with a liner; medium warm, take a raincoat without the liner; and warm, take a cardigan sweater. People also wonder what to wear to the airport going from cold to hot weather. A raincoat will do nicely. Think about it — you really aren't outside at the airport after you arrive in your car. Go for an easy mix-and-match color scheme. And keep it light — one suitcase on wheels and a carry-on.

Make sure all prescriptions, cosmetics, toiletries, and travel documents are in your carry-on. Also, bring a change of underwear and a bathing suit if you are heading somewhere warm. You can always buy a little coverup and thongs if the airline loses your luggage, and you can sleep in your underwear the first night if you have to.

A frequent flyer, Debby Russo, suggests packing a large nylon folding duffle bag in your suitcase. As you accumulate souvenirs at the end of the trip, throw all the dirty laundry and shoes into the nylon bag, and you will have plenty of room for all those bargains that were so hard to resist.

Businessmen who travel frequently keep an overnight carry-on bag packed at all times with a clean shirt, change of underwear, and toiletries. The better organized you are, the better the flight.

Remove all old luggage tags, and make sure new ones have the flight number and destination on them. Be sure to put your name, address, and telephone number inside the bag in case your tags fall off.

A WORD ABOUT EASTERN EUROPE...

The welcome mat is out in Eastern Europe, and many travelers are eager to visit Poland, Hungary, Romania, Czechoslovakia, East Germany, and Bulgaria. To hear a recorded summary of travel advisories, call (202) 647-5225.

The State Department publishes a pamphlet (*Tips for Travels to Eastern Europe and Yugoslavia*), pamphlet 044-00002176-5. It can be ordered by sending $1 to the U. S. Government Printing Office, Washington, D.C. 20402.

Chapter Six

Flying with Others

TAKE MY WIFE, **PLEASE!**

FLYING WITH CHILDREN

When asked, "Do you like children," who was it that replied, "Sure, with lots of barbecue sauce"? You may feel that way when traveling with kids, but after trying some of these tips, you might be surprised — with a little ingenuity, taking the kids can turn into a great family experience.

If you are flying with a baby, tell the airlines when you are making reservations that you will be traveling with an infant. During takeoff and landing, you will be instructed to hold your baby in your arms and to place the seatbelt around both of you.

Most airlines are equipped with baby kits, which contain baby powder, disposable diapers (not many), a bowl, a spoon, and baby food. Bring along extra milk or juice for takeoff and landing. Baby's ears will adjust to the change in air pressure by taking a few swallows. Milk is available on planes, but if the baby needs formula, bring enough for the whole flight (the baby kit doesn't have any). Flight attendants will warm bottles, but they don't have time to mix formula for you. Also, pack plenty of diapers and resealable plastic bags for disposing of dirty diapers.

My friend Robin suggests that if your child is a little older, make sure you bring along a favorite toy. It will help the child feel a little more secure. And, if you are taking school-aged children with you, buy them a book about the part of the United States or foreign country you are on your way to visit. Get them feeling involved about plans for the upcoming trip — for example, let them pick a restaurant. (Hope they don't pick the Ritz!)

KIDS WHO ARE FLYING ALONE

The airlines will allow children over the age of five to travel alone, but you must notify the airline when you make the reservation. The airlines will want to know the name, address, and phone number of the person who brings the child to the airport, and the same information about the person who will meet the child at the destination.

When you bring a child who is traveling alone to the airport, ask for a passenger service rep to assist you during check-in and boarding. Even with help, however, you are responsible for making sure the child gets to the right gate and is seated on the right plane.

Some service is provided at the destination end. Again, inform the passenger service rep at the destination airport that the child will be traveling alone, and the rep will make sure the child is met by the appropriate person.

HANDICAPPED PEOPLE

Handicapped people are now adding a new dimension to their lives. Because of the close air transportation network, a handicapped person can travel safely and efficiently.

Before a handicapped person boards the plane, a customer service rep will notify the passenger service staff of the nature of the handicap so they will be prepared to offer the right type of assistance. If any special diet is required, the rep will notify the commissaries.

Handicapped passengers who have their own lightweight folding wheelchairs can take them (free of charge) aboard the plane. Passengers who can stand can be escorted to the lavatories. If they cannot stand, they should have a friend accompany them.

Qualified personnel will be notified of a handicapped person's arrival at the destination end of the flight and will be prepared to offer any type of assistance that is necessary — for example, wheelchairs to help get to connecting flights.

Remember, if you are handicapped and have any questions about flying, the airlines recommend that you first ask your doctor and then inform the airline so special arrangements can be made if necessary.

FLYING IF YOU ARE PREGNANT

Medical authorities claim that flying has no harmful effects on a normal pregnancy. Most airlines accept expectant mothers as passengers up to and including the thirty-fifth week of pregnancy.

Some airlines will accept pregnant women after that time for short trips, providing a doctor's certificate is furnished stating that the woman has been examined and found to be physically able to fly.

Major airlines give their cabin attendants the necessary training in first aid in the event of a premature birth.

OLDER FOLKS

Age is no reason to deny yourself fun in the sun. In fact, doctors say the environment of today's pressurized airplane cabin is ideal for the older traveler. According to the American Medical Association, older people with well-compensated cardiovascular and respiratory systems tolerate flight excellently. Folks with high blood pressure and even asthma aren't bothered by plane trips.

Most people with heart ailments are able to fly without worrying about aggravating their condition, provided they're able to manage ordinary physical activity without problems, such as undue fatigue, palpitations, shortness of breath, or chest pain.

Advise the airline when you book your flight if you have any type of physical handicap so the airline can make special arrangements to accommodate you.

FLYING WITH PETS

Airlines will transport household pets, but certain handling standards must be observed to ensure that your pet will be carried safely. A pet must be carried in the proper container. If you don't have a pet carrier, the airlines will provide you with one at a modest cost, roughly between $20 and $45. Pet carriers are available in four sizes, depending on the weight and breed of the animal.

You will need a health certificate from your vet before an airline will accept your pet for transport. You might also ask the vet about tranquilizers — they might help your pet travel quietly and calmly. Be sure and feed your animal a light meal prior to flight time, and don't give too much water. The airlines will advise you about the paperwork required if your pet is traveling alone on an overseas flight. You will need a U.S. customs shippers declaration, a vet's health certificate, and a rabies vaccination certificate. These forms are available from the airlines.

The airlines will also provide you with booklets that describe different countries' entrance requirements for your pet. Air freight rates are based on total weight and volume of the pet, plus the container. These rates apply only when the pet travels alone. When the pet accompanies you, the rate is the same as for excess baggage.

FLYING WITH WHITE-KNUCKLED FLYERS

If you're flying with a fearful flyer, be prepared to be a sounding board a week before the flight — the time when nervous tension starts to build up.

Help your fearful flyer pack and get ready way ahead of time. Suggest the relaxation techniques in this book (they really do work). Talk about safety statistics when you board the plane and try to hold hands, especially during takeoff and landing. These are the scariest times for a fearful flyer, and a large dose of reassurance from you — your conversation, your hand-holding, and so forth will be a great comfort.

Just as phobics come in all sizes, shapes, and varieties, there is no one "garden variety" of white-knuckled flyer. Therefore, there is no one special way to deal with the white-knuckled flyer. Although I do have several suggestions on how to help, take your cue from your fearful companion. There is no logic to the way white-knuckled flyers act; one minute they might want to interact with others and another minute they might want to be left alone. Here are my suggestions:

- Do not take lightly or make fun of your companion's fears. One person's phobia is another's fantasy.
- Try to get the white-knuckled flyer interested in the movie, a book or magazine, conversation, or even some of the banter offered through the headsets.
- If you want to play amateur psychologist, try to get your white-knuckled friend to talk about his or her fears. Focus on the logical and rational aspects of the flight.
- Back off if your white-knuckled flyer just wants to be left alone. Many do.
- Just be there. Be ready to offer whatever your fearful companion wants, whether it be a hand to hold or a hand of cards.

Chapter Seven

Flying Phobias

GOOD NEWS — HELP IS AVAILABLE!

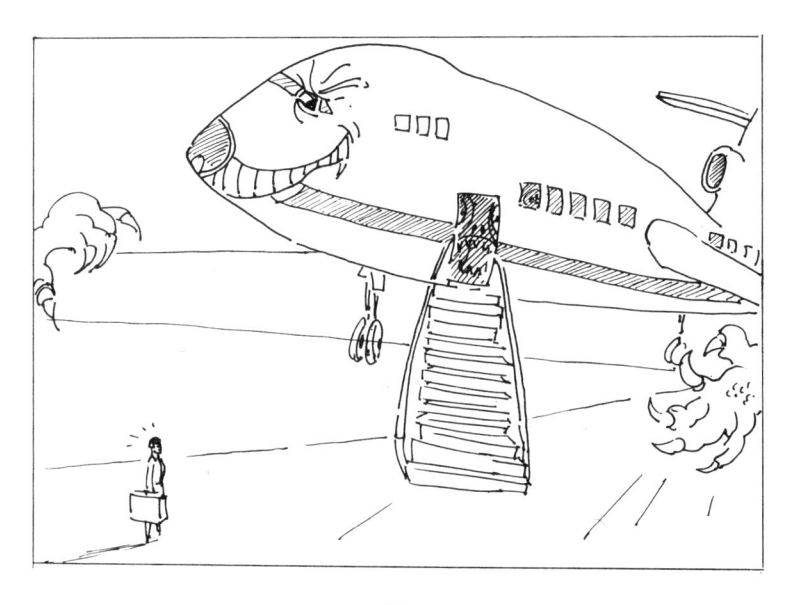

A phobia is a severe emotional reaction to a situation that poses no real threat to life or safety and doesn't produce panic in nonphobic people. Because the terror and panic are so great, the phobic person avoids the fear-producing situation — in this case, airplanes. The fear of fear itself becomes so overwhelming that the phobic person avoids planes altogether.

Phobias are often responses to panic attacks. According to Dr. Forgione at the Institute for Psychology of Air Travel, in many cases the panic attacks are triggered by a physical condition called panic disorder. The condition begins with repeated panic episodes or irrational terror, with symptoms such as sweating, heart palpitations, chest discomfort, shortness of breath, choking sensations, faintness, trembling, tingling, hot or cold flashes, feeling of unreality, fear of losing control, fear of dying, and fear of going crazy.

If you avoid planes because you are phobic, you are not alone. The good news is that professional, qualified help is available. Believe me, I understand your fear. I'm an ex-phobic, and I know from experience there are ways to overcome it. Most phobics are intelligent, creative, and very "normal" people, so don't put yourself down as unintelligent, uncreative, or "weird."

The following therapists and phobia clinics deal with the fear of flying. I am certain that one of them can help you!

Glen Arnold
Thairapy
4500 Campus Drive, Suite 628F
Newport Beach, CA 92660
(714) 756-1133

Atlanta Phobia and Anxiety Clinic
5555 Peachtree Dunwoody Road
Suite 106
Atlanta, GA 30342
(404) 256-9325

Shirley S. Babior, L.C.S.W.
Center for Anxiety and Stress Treatment
4295 Ibis Street
San Diego, CA 92103
(619) 543-0510

9555 Genesee Ave., Suite 202
La Jolla, CA 92121
(619) 458-1066

June Blackburn
Fear of Flying Clinic
15127 N.E. 24th, Suite 211
Redmond, WA 988052-5530
(206) 772-1122

Capt. T.W. Cummings
The Program for the Fearful Flyer
2021 Country Club Prado
Coral Gables, FL 33134
(305) 261-7042

Ron M. Doctor, Ph.D.
Freedom To Fly
941 Westwood Boulevard, Suite 237
Los Angeles, Calif. 90024
(213) 208-7577

Albert G. Forgione, Ph.D.
Institute for Psychology of Air Travel
25 Huntington Ave., Suite 300
Boston, MA 02116
(617) 437-1811
(Home Study Course also available)

Dr. Jorge H. DeNapoli
Andover Phobic Clinic
166 N. Main Street
Andover, MA 01810
(508) 475-7249

Fear of Flying Clinic
1777 Borel Place, Room 300
San Mateo, CA 94402
(415) 341-1595

Carol Cott Gross
Travel & Fly without Fear
310 Madison Avenue
New York, NY 10017
(212) 697-7666

Joe Mallet, Ph.D.
Phobia Treatment Center of Chevy Chase
2 Wisconsin Circle, Suite 700
Chevy Chase, MD 20815
(301) 654-3565

John A. Moran, Ph.D.
Cleared for Takeoff
3337 N. Miller Road, Suite 105
Scottsdale, AZ 85251
(602) 994-9773

Carol Stauffer M.S.W. & Capt. Frank Petee
U.S. Air Fearful Flyers Program
Box 100
Glenshaw, PA 15116
(412) 366-8112

Flying Without Fear
School of Professional Psychology
Wright State University
Dayton, OH 45435

Phobia Treatment Center of Columbia
2000 Century Plaza Suite 311
Columbia, MD 21044

SOAR (Seminars On Aeroanxiety Relief)
P.O. Box 747
Westport, CT 06881
(800) 332-7359

For additional Phobia Information contact:
Phobia Society of America
133 Rolins Ave., Suite 4B
Rockville, MD
(301) 231-9350

Edie,
I know someone who would love this book!
Please send me _____ copies of

Flying Can Be Fun

A GUIDE FOR THE WHITE-KNUCKLED FLYER

I am enclosing $ _____ .
($6.95 per book plus $1.50 postage and handling)

> *Send cash, check, or money order, payable to:*
> **DYENAMIKS, INC.**
> **P.O. Box 733**
> **Middleton, MA 01949**
> *Sorry, no C.O.D.   Allow 4 weeks for delivery.*

Please mail my books to:

NAME _____

STREET _____

CITY _____ STATE _____ ZIP _____